Koestler Voices: New Poetry from Prisons, Vol. 4

With a foreword by Joelle Taylor
Edited by Beth Aydon and Esther Sorooshian

First published in the UK in 2023 by Koestler Arts,
170 Du Cane Road, London W12 0TX.

ISBN 978-1-3999-6438-8

Design by Polimekanos

Koestler Voices: New Poetry from Prisons

With a foreword by Joelle Taylor
Edited by Beth Aydon and Esther Sorooshian

Vol. 4

Bookend I

Warmest Place

A Crow's Caw from the Throat of a Swan

Interstellar Soup

A Expect Maer

Bookend II

Introduction

Welcome to the fourth volume of *Koestler Voices*.

These past two years have been filled with change and excitement at Koestler Arts. We celebrated our sixtieth anniversary with our biggest exhibition ever, filling our usual space at the Southbank Centre with over 1,850 artworks, curated by the internationally renowned artist Ai Weiwei. So far, 2023 has been another busy year, with more than 8,000 artworks entered into the Koestler Awards and our move to a new, more environmentally friendly, accessible building. In April our former chief executive retired, and I stepped into the role. The charity owes thanks to Sally Taylor for eight years of innovations, including founding this poetry anthology which brings such joy and inspiration to so many.

For the first time, *Koestler Voices* has been edited in-house. The team's editorial approach has been informed by years of working with the thousands of artworks and entrants that have embarked on a journey with Koestler Arts. Many thanks to the poets for sharing their words, and to the editors Beth Aydon and Esther Sorooshian for bringing them together. Beth and Esther used their instinct for good writing and understanding of what matters to our entrants in order to select the forty-five works reproduced here from some 2,000 entries submitted into the Poetry and Poetry Collection Koestler Awards categories. Each prison library will receive a copy from us through our Anthology Crowdfunder, to make sure people in prisons are able to be inspired by this work as readers and future contributors.

We thank the T. S. Eliot foundation and our crowd-funder supporters for their donations that allowed the anthology to come to life. Thanks are to be extended to the rest of the Koestler Arts team for their continued work through these busy years, and in particular to Phoebe Dunn, Mali Clements, Tilly Buckroyd, Stephanie Weber, and our copyeditor Ed Wall, for their contributions to this publication.

I'm delighted that one of my first tasks as chief executive was to get our team started on Volume 4 – it is humbling to read the heartfelt, brave works that have been entrusted to us, and to be able to share them with the public.

Fiona Curran
Chief Executive

Foreword

'True creativity starts where language ends'
– *Arthur Koestler*

Books are many things. Some are mirrors in which we
hunt our true reflections. Others are windows which
allow the reader to observe the small rituals of living
as if through the glass walls of a vitrine. This book is
a door.

Writing is a kind of freedom, a rush of air against
the face. It allows us to journey to impossible places,
to reverse time, to rewrite the past and reimagine the
future. It is the essence of travel. We can explore the
world as seen through a square window of white paper.
And we can take the most challenging and beautiful
journey of all: that which leads us back to ourselves.

The contributors to this anthology have travelled
far. They have found their voice in their hands. And
it sings.

While it can be argued that all writing responds to
the idea of hope, there is of course a deep grief that
circles the book like crows above a playground as the
authors consider a life of loss: of family, of children;
even the loss of a reflection the writer recognises.
Memory takes the place of photographs, of touch. But
in the writing, connection is remade. Old wounds are
cauterised and begin to heal. This is poetry as intimate
cinema, poetry as witness, as prayer. As such there is
a miracle to these writings, a strange belonging found
only at the rub of a pen against paper.

This anthology is many things. It is a map of thinking
that traces the journey from 'an age before anxiety' to
the search for an identity in an institution whose sole

purpose is to remove it. It contemplates the 'geometry of living', the mathematics of survival, before letting out a crow's caw from a swan's throat. One writer tells us simply, 'I searched my heart / and found a flower' – and perhaps that is the true force of these collected works. A book that is a mirror, a window, a door, a map, bright petals pushing through snow. It is poetry that is living, that pushes against the margins of the page, a wild animal of a book. I offer my sincere thanks to the writers of this collection and to all the people who have stood behind each contributor to make their work possible, to make it shine.

Poetry is an international language. It speaks to us in images, in small cinema, in body, and in memory. You don't need to understand a poem in order to understand it. It is a feeling thing, an idea dropped by one writer and picked up in the street by another.

This book is testament to the invaluable work of creative writing tutors and resident poets across the criminal justice system. It is testament to librarians and education managers who prise workshops into the tight prison schedule, each session an introduction to a different kind of freedom: the writing and sharing of original work, the unpicking of famous poems, the learning of form and craft.

When you open the door to this book, stand back and let the humanity rush past you.

Joelle Taylor

Bookend I

The Pen

To fall for the pen
Is to live with your
                    heart outside
Of your chest.
In-hand, the eternal
Sanguine ink spurts with
Each
Beat
Of
Inspiration.

Warmest Place

Untitled

Wen I got locked you couldn't look me in da eye
Sorry mom for da times you cried
For the times I got locked and I know you tried
Didn't change ma ways from time I don't know why
I know we still cool and I love you loads
All the good days that we had I send a toast
If I blow wid this rap you're da first 2 get post
I know you care mom you always done da most
Runnin round the house causing trouble
You was always around 2 give me a cuddle
Memba my first pair of wellies jumpin in puddles
And da big teddy bear I had called him snuggles
Make sure you know ima always love you
Plus my little bros I love them 2
I'm away right now but I'll be home soon
Ima try make it out and shine like the moon

Cardiff City Stadium

As you walk into the stadium and the feeling just hits,
You see all the boys in their blue-and-white kits,
As the feeling comes and you walk down the stairs,
And the wild supporter whips out his blue flares,
The nation chanting and people ranting,

As Sheyi Ojo tackles the ball,
Into the net with a header from Joe Ralls,
The bluebirds going insane as they cheer,
Blue flags, insults and strong beer,
Bartley Bluebird skipping with joy,
Finally not a new manager to employ,
As Joel Bagan makes a tackle,
Causes Swansea fans to ramshackle,

I can't get enough of Cardiff City football,
It is the best team anyone can recall,
The capital of Wales, the biggest and the best,
Far better than Swansea, Bristol and all the rest,
Cardiff fans are the loyalest ever,
We sit through 4–0s, 3–0s, and whatever,
But that doesn't matter my heart will never change,
I'm a bluebird till I die or that would just be strange.

Cinquain

Behind
to leave a sound
prison done prison done
surviving path motivation
own life

A sound
no addiction
alcohol and/or drugs
recovery recovery
goal goal

Should Have Took a Picture

Got up at 7,
Showered and ate by 8,
On the train by 9,
Rushing too much.
Busy trains,
People talking,
Chat chat, clack clack, tap tap,

Central Station.
Pinks, blues,
Hues,
Pictures on station walls,
People in suits,
Smells of oil, dust.

Burning Big Macs,
Diet coke,
Travelling on a grey train to London,
Should have took a picture.
Going to see my pharaoh on the wall,
My latest, greatest, painting; the best of them all.

Thank goodness!
We're off the train,
Fast trains,
I don't like.
Should have took a picture.

Black cab to see Big Ben chiming at 1,
Watching the river while walking along,
Should have took a picture.

Laughing with the pharaoh,
Seeing my picture on the Southbank wall,
Paul, Eric, Tracy and me,
In three and a half hours we painted the town,
Enjoying the day.
Should have took a picture

I did take a picture,
It's all here in my mind,
A memory of one day,
One day in my life.

Black and White

I look into the photo, the memories swirl.
I must have been three or possibly four.
After that our mum had gone out of the door.
My sister holds my hand, all is okay.

Mum wiping the dirt from my face, it needs to be clean.
A bowl placed on my head, I wriggle like a worm.
The click clack of the scissors at work as I squirm.
My sister holds my hand, all is okay.

My sister and me are sat side by side.
I fiddle with my tie, it was navy blue.
I wonder why the photo only features us two?
My sister holds my hand, all is okay.

The thumb I suck is pulled from my mouth.
The photographer tries to make me laugh I'm sure.
I am a shy child, so I look at the floor.
My sister holds my hand, all is okay.

Why was it taken, who was it for?
It feels heavy in my hand and weighs on my mind.
My memories are so hard to unwind.
My sister holds my hand, all is okay.

Not Long...

I'm not there to get you dressed,
I'm not there to put you to bed,
I'm not there to wipe your tears,
I'm not there to chase away your fears.
I'm missing out on so much, you're growing
so fast and I miss your tiny touch.
You're going to parties, you're going to school,
when I get home you're gonna be so tall.
You're being so strong, you're being so brave,
I'm so sorry our lives have turned out
this way.
The guilt I carry kills me inside but I have
to stay strong for all our lives.
Nanny will give you so much love and
grandad will give you millions of hugs.
You will stay at their house and have your
own room, you will have lots of laughs
and mummy will be home soon.
It won't be long till I can get you dressed,
It won't be long till I can put you to bed,
It won't be long till I can hold you tight,
It won't be long till I can kiss you
    goodnight.

My Literacy Mentee

My literacy mentee
Folder bursting with words and ink
He's been given a 'special pen'

I recall long-forgotten quotes
'There's a rat in separate'
'One collar two socks'
'Abundant ants'

Never before have I appreciated
The glorious ampersand
Inquisitive curve of a question mark
And extravagant 'g'

He laughs whilst we work
Telling me jokes
And the latest plot in Emmerdale
What's a semi colon do? he asks
(good question)

But then
a transfer
D cat
a quick farewell in the servery queue

Now when I write
I think of him
Spelling 'beautifully'
With his special pen.

Nana's

I sat by the fire
but that wasn't the warmest place
in your home.
That place always moved
That place
was you

Ash

I made Dad an ashtray.
With space for six cigs,
In a year that followed
Mid-morning milk, naps
And dungarees;
An age before anxiety, girls
And Levi's jeans.
In days as long as Silly String,
Our teacher gave us clay,
To bring forth a thing
From grey matter,
As slate sky is moulded
By a tearaway ray.
With coaxing pressure
And thumbscrews
Of hesitant little hands,
I kneaded the memories
Of its ever-shifting form,
Building up a rise;
The inescapable fall.
As minds bounded only
By grass house walls,
Made a spewing volcano
And fearsome dragon's head,
I could not escape
The falling ash.
Or was it, beyond the embers,
That I wished the poor man
Dead?

Glen

Mad as a box of hatters,
Daft as a sausage-meat pen.
A succinct and concise description
Of my old wing-mate, Glen

Goldfish

I wish I was a goldfish
with nothing in my head
a thirty-second memory
from birth until I'm dead
no regrets to haunt me
no echoes of the past
whatever ills befall me
the pain will never last.

I'd be a tiny goldfish
and swim around my bowl
every lap a new one
a forever spotless soul
as a fish, I know I'd smile
I'm sure I'd smile a lot
exciting new adventures
the last one soon forgot.

I wish I was a goldfish
with nothing in my head
but every day I think of you
from breakfast until bed.

DE-MEN-T-I-A

DE, DE, DE, DE, what is that word again?

There goes the click, door opening.

Next I'm in a chair with wheels going for
my medicine.

MEN, MEN, Men, Men, who are they, I think
I know some of them, but where from, I do not
know.

Sat in a room, not very big, just myself
feeling alone in my own little world.

Tea, Tea, Tea, Tea, my friend has made me
a cuppa, he is the one who helps me with
everything I do.

There are times when I can remember events
from years gone by and the next it seems
like a dream.

I, I, I, I, wish I could think on, what is
real and what is not?

Mealtimes come, first dinner then tea, my
friend brings them to me, smile on face.

The door closes, there goes the click.

Alone, Alone, Alone, Alone, in my own little world
trying to remember that special word.

This Place

We serve this sentence together.
Against a landscape.
Our shoulder blades held high.
Under autumnal colour,
Or smothered in summer sky

Mountains they surround us.
But I never feel hemmed in.
I paint them with my eyes,
And draw them closer in.

Still, I get up in the morning.
There is always something to do.
And I think about this place a lot,
When I think about you.

A Crow's Caw from
the Throat of
a Swan

Kaleidoscope

Through chaos, form, and function,
A brave new world glimmers fleeting.
Hidden through a lens unfocused,
The geometry of the living appears.

A Non-Verbal Artist Prepares a Work

There is a circularity,
a galaxy bound in tape
and paper and strips of cloth.
A tight layered ball.

A parcel containing mysteries,
an unknown world of darkness
that fears what it cannot control;
what it cannot imprison.

Many layers of paper,
of leather and textile,
of string and sticky tape
and cardboard-sided enclosures,

layers of time and experience,
fulfilment and failure,
birth, pain, ragged loss –
coverings from a long life.

And, deep in the middle,
past all the wrappings,
all the seals and glue,
at the centre – the whisper

of a different voice

Sky

Sometimes I lie on the grass
and watch the clouds in the sky,
feel the sun on my face,
listen to the seagulls.

I close my eyes,
and there could be a glass of wine just out of reach.
But this is not the same sky,
and these are not the right seagulls.

Transitioning the Gendered Mind

Seeing Her discomforts
my sense of Him –
arousing distress,
or a confused self –
vision of one, replaced,
by knowledge of a deeper truth,
that lies unwantingly known
in the half shadow of my mind.

He moves like She,
emitting sounds that jar –
a Crow's caw from
the throat of a Swan –
I dare not look, directly –
wanting to see without looking,
or being seen to look,
as if in looking it is I
which is exposed –
misunderstanding self,
and self's inherence.

Men with breasts scare in a way that confuses –
and so fear paralyses my vocal chords
    as if I am alien to myself.

To Feel Autumn

Written at HMP Downview (5 p.m.) after spending ten minutes barefoot soaking up the earth's energy and immersing myself in nature's loving embrace.

There's a fizz that's running dizzily
channelling through my blood
I can feel my nostrils flaring
as my brain receives the flood.

The grass, the earth, the falling leaves
arrive separately, not together
the hairs on arms seem each to touch
separate elements of the weather.

The symphony of nature's sounds
I hear as individual parts
percussive winds speak to my soul
wagtails chirp into my heart.

Beneath my feet, below the ground,
nature drums a steady beat
my hand that rests upon the tree
touches life flow in retreat.

Filled with rich, emotive truth
the wheel is turning once again
as autumn claims this time as mine
to blaze with colour through my reign.

I feel each microbe of my being
drowning happily in a sentient bath
and burst with Disney rays of light
as the wheel transforms me on my path.

I prepare for sacred time that comes
filled with the love that shall remain
and honour all, with prayer for strength
to embrace the future, come this Samhain.

Felon to Freedom

F orget Freedom
E very Second
L ife for a life when you pick up a knife
O bscene Sentences
N ever did I think

T orturous
O rdeal

F ree Mindset
R elieved
E ver will I think
E motional Path
D idn't think
O nly acted
My Journey

Adagio

The sunshine's gone. A clear day was all I needed.
It's easier to shop, to look and browse
– others' leftovers are enough to divert the mind:
slightly battered books with stains and yellowing pages;
CDs and DVDs that need examining for scratches –
but today I am undiverted and alone in here,
out of the wind and lashing rain,
with some music and my thoughts and the old
unanswered questions. The same mysteries
between the lines we lived to play from the beginning.
Out there, still so unreadable, you are you. I am me.
I can get no further. Is this how it goes?
I can't drink tea from your cup today. Still
I can't give it away. Empty and clean now,
it sits, hid in the back of the cupboard.

The Trainer That Sat Next to the Trainer

One night my white Nike trainer
spoke to my other white Nike trainer
the right one said to the left one

Hollo: I'm your neighbour and also your brother.

I've been meaning to say hi for a while
but did not want to alarm the occupant
of this cell in case he heard us
converse.

The other one extended his lace
they both held hands throughout the night.

When morning come they both went their
separate ways one to the left the other to the right.

Almost Normal

Written after a day at hospital.

It was almost normal. I went outside today to
Fix that which was broken at A and E.
Of sea glass skies I felt the white
Heat on my skin, but no warmth touched me.
There were lives lived. And I thought how
Long it had been since I last saw
Children swallow daisy-chains like my
Years, their lungs filled with spring.
>The breakfast table cleared, nectarines of youth
>bruised,
>The noon of my life done, a languid post-lunch
>laze ensued.
It was almost normal.

A lady walks her dog, her coat like
Crumpled cigar ash, but the cherry of her face
Glows anew, eyes meet soul, and she lifts
Her cheeks like morning sun. She'd recognised
The joy her dog had brought. And I
Wondered in the car if she'd refund her
Look if she knew my lot. Oh how
Long it's been since I last saw
>Life that lives for day and night
>And falls to sleep, not wakes in fright.
It was almost normal.

Crumpled papers grew in unshorn grass, like
Buds of thought that spring had passed,
And ink-soaked soil crumbled like rotten cork.
So strange to see ideas not bloom
And left to our world like littered clay
Untouched by kiln or midnight flame. For
Here our thoughts congest the air,
Recycled acrid fumes from cars,
 And in our grey garage we drink with thirst,
 Petrol thoughts to our last day from our first.
It was almost normal.

Then lights I saw, like neon dreams
That throb in my heart like Vegas gleams.
Pink corals blushed, apricot hues that bled,
Like swans into shadows blue on silver lakes;
Yet like youth that drinks the skies to indigo
Black, the bulbs shine on, strange hangovers
Of life's day-to-day, as if to say that
'We were here.' So long it's been since I last saw
 Proof of life run like scars, or move like dew
 On an insect's back, or like mists on waters stew.
It was almost normal.

a prisoner

nothing depends
upon

a prisoner

and that's what
hurts

so much
I think

Birds

I hear birds in the night
Calling out for their loves
Blackbirds with hearts as pure
As a pair of silk white doves.

Interstellar
Soup

Claire

In class I sit next to a girl
Who happens to be called Claire Voyance
She talks through every lesson
And has become an unbearable annoyance.
Our teacher Mr Short
Has a temper that suits his name
And with pieces of chalk (or the duster)
He has impeccable aim.
Claire was busy gassing
As Mr Short took off his shoe
Once launched, it hit her forehead (and I said)
'You didn't see that coming, did you?'

Hotel Review

Soap worn to a nose
In profile on a soap dish
Too hot water stings
Too rough towel scrapes
Too much steam stymies
The drying process.

Waking eyes treated
To the Bricklayer's art
A missed morning call
A teapot lukewarm
And through my brain
Next door's TV crawls.

A bouncy castle, backache bed
A clog dance ceiling song
Too much heat
Too little space
Going home tomorrow.
Damn.

Zoography

Paris was a peacock
blocking every view with its beauty
of Haussmann's order and uniform shutters
drawing the eyes from gutters and rodents.

New Orleans was a cobra
hidden on branches dripping with Spanish moss
or flaring its blaring pageant hood and rictus
grinning for revellers.

West Berlin was a cockatiel
strutting garishly around its cage
loud and confident but always
keeping one eye on the door.

East Berlin was a black cat
preferring to appear fleetingly between streetlights
beneath or behind the wall, before
slipping into shadows where I might follow.

New York was a puppy
chasing its tail around the Empire State Building
'til it became a blur of noise and movement
tugging at me to follow it in circles.

London was an oyster
guarding its pearl against currents
washed in on the Thames
letting me see its treasure rarely.

Rome was a tortoise
carrying its shell of ruins and memories

along the Appian Way
ignoring the blue smog of progress.

Luxor was a crocodile
drifting languidly on the Nile
basking peacefully, but with beady eyes
watching and ready to lash out at weakness.

Prison was a snail
slowly retreating into hidden quarters
antennae prone for any change in the air
trapped in its fragile shell, endlessly biding its time.

Absconding Humanity

She was scared of the darkness
So she became it
She was also scared of people
But she never became one of those

Happiness is...

Syncopation, Laser lights, Driving in the Driving
Rain, Smiling eyes, coffee, pastry, empty roads, Pastry,
Bargain Hunt, Collectable Decimal Coins, Lists, The
Noise of Swaying Trees, The smell of wet Tarmac,
Alpha-Numeric order, Mazurkas, Waltzes, Franz
Liszt, Method-Man, Bovril, Marmite, Chopsticks,
Calculus, Waterfalls, Biscuits, Journeys in the front
seat on the top of a double decker bus, headphones,
Spotify, Hot chilli peppers, Tender Lamb, YouTube,
My MOTHER'S Hug, Family gatherings, extravagant
clothes, The Colour purple, Fresh Linen, chocolate
mousse, The Chase, A hot Shower, Fixtures and
Fittings, hand tools, Sudoku, Logic problems, small
kittens, taking off my socks when home, An Ice cold
bottle of water, Quantum Mechanics, Architecture,
Fried chicken, Punctuation, The Noise of a Library,
Oxymorons, chip shop chips, super hot baked beans,
cheese on toast, Salt, Bananas, dripping with butter
crumpets, drum and bass, Dusk, Raves, Operas, comedy
clubs, needlework, Auctions, Aimless wandering,
Map Reading, Etymology, car boot sales, Watching a
Farmer sow/plough a field, window shopping, Starling
murmuration, Front Diastemas, Pareidolia, London,
Brighton, Sausages, Lego, C#, Fermi's Paradox, Eye
shadow, Basslines, Violins, Green Eyes, Typewriters,
Wallpapering, D.I.Y, helicopters, Rolling a cigarette,
baking, Cooking, Honesty, Holograms, Manners,
opening a letter, A Quiz, Finishing a Book

Identity

I WALKED DOWN THE STREET AND I FOLLOWED
MY FEET

STRAIGHT PAST THE SHOP, ROUND THE CORNER
– I WILL NOT STOP

THERE WAS A MAN, IN FRONT OF ME, HE
STARED WHICH MADE ME STOP.

THE MAN SAID HELLO, HAVEN'T SEEN YOU FOR
A WHILE,

I BOWED MY HEAD, HE STARTED TO SMILE, HOW
ARE YOU JOHN AND HOW IS YOUR WIFE?

I HAVEN'T GOT ONE – NO TROUBLE AND STRIFE.
BESIDES WHICH MY NAME'S NOT JOHN, YOU
KNOW. AND, I REALLY MUST BE GETTING ON.

SO CHEERIO I SAID TO THE STRANGE YOUNG
MAN AND I HOPED I WOULD SEE HIM AGAIN
ONE DAY NOW HE KNOWS WHO I AM.

International Space Station

I am no god but I have a God's eye view
I'm just a service utility with a mechanical eye.
I watch, as night and day pull at the
covers of the shared marital bed. I could
pretend at God, for I hear talk. Considerations
of collective fate, the cycle cannot be broken,
cast adrift in cold unremitting night. I'm just
an eye as the beast is there for burden, my
masters, unsettled by eerie deep space
silence of science-fiction's facts, no
persistent drone of propulsion no pistons
no moving parts, I know, for I hear talk.
Talk of sentiment, cry-play, wound-laugh,
tradition-superstition. I watch their world,
my solar-panelled phalanx silvered by the
sun and circle the fragile biosphere, eyes keened
on the spherical motherboard of wriggling
striving bio-organisms, an ever-spinning
snow globe of white windswept lather and
blue briny deep. The veins of Himalayan
range, familiar as raised tributaries on the
back of a hand. And what of God? God was
pleased with his handiwork, I know, for I
hear talk whilst tracing the taper of a comet's
trail. Forever floating where nature ends
and sequined cosmos begins, wearing a
groove in the passage of ageless wandering.
Through flawless glass iris, pointillist
clusters of iridescence minutely glitter
like a starling's folded wing. I scan the barcodes
and braille of human behaviour, their horrors

and hopes copulate beneath the microscope.
Much is feared little is said of intergalactic
extinction events. All, a shimmering haze
far reaching fingers of unseen ultra-violet,
ultra-violent solar flare, elliptical galaxies
happily accidental, an ever expanding
interstellar soup.

Initial Impressions of a Variety of Mugshots in Four Words

Calm pensive

Very embarrassed

Looks like

Don't mess

Covid mask

I shouldn't

Deer in

Is that

Rock star

Feeling sorry

Quite impressive

Laughing his

Is that

and	thoughtful
and	ashamed
mainly	indifference
with	me
under	chin
be	here
the	headlights
a	smirk?
in	training
for	himself
facial	hair
head	off
a	tear?

Swarfega Soap

You bad boy!
Blue words spill forth with affluence,
Staining our ears and cheeks with undiluted pink.
Sandpapered violet.
Velvet couldn't soften this.
Swarfega soap could help.
But we've tried that,
and it seems he likes the taste.

A Expect Maer

A Piece N Jam Waein

A wunner wut that tastes like?
Thae seem tae sell it so we'll n so delicious;
Yae can almost feel it trickle doon yir gullet n in tae
    yir stomach;
Ma mooths waterin' joost thinkin' aboot it.

Tae me this is joost anither delayed ir postponed
    action,
As ah procrastinate aboot food n drinks;
That a can only imagine the noo.

Am a waein fae poverty n hardship: stunted;
In a rough environment; a rough up bringin' wae yer
    consequential Rucksack o
Circumstances ye cerry wae ye.

'A wunner wut that tastes like?' is the story o ma life;
A WANT; A DESIRE; A EXPECT MAER.

It's a luck o the draw at times,
But thirs' yin thing fir shaer a'v niver loast
    ma appetite,
Fir ivrithin' n maer; ivrithin' that's no shite,
    Sum o that 'Gucci stuff'.

Oh... how the ather half live... n thae depressin'
    advertisements man!
Life can bae so unfair fir the yins' withoot thir fair
    share.

An Interview

The refugee boys answered the Home
    Office's inquisitor:

my land has no gardens
no flowers
just sea, dust and flats

my sky has plenty of stars
and bees.[1]
Bees – killing the sweetest things in my life
and all of those who call me honey...

they searched our houses
i searched my heart
and found a flower

i told no one lest they hear
i plucked it
cursed it
then I chucked it into the sea

---

1. Drones.

Plastic Fantastic?

Plastic Fantastic?
It was fantastic for those in the business.
For as we entered the throw-away age,
they climbed up the Forbes rich list.
They'd knew about non-degradable
and what that really meant for ages,
but greedy no good money grabbers,
don't mind being bastards in the history pages,
and history's what we'll be as time runs oot,
yet still there's the climate change deniers
who just don't give a flying hoot.

Plastic fantastic?
It's not enough just to fill coloured bins.
Just as I'm sure going to church
wouldn't absolve the religious of all their sins.
So our governments need to act now.
Not just grasp for bins, absolution and votes.
For if the powers that be don't get it right,
it's all of us missing the lifeboats.
So it's time to take a stand.
No navel gazing, stuttering, muttering excuses.
Micro-plastic the line drawn in the sand.

Plastic fantastic?
Aye that's right. Let it sink in.
Us that would do anything for our weans.
Yet here we are, heads in the sand,
leaving it to them to face the coming pains.
Think about all the innocents in the world

righting the wrongs of our selfish making.
Shameful and cruel we are, as how easy
their futures we've knowingly taken.

Plastic Fantastic?
I bet whoever coined that phrase,
like CFCs and lead in your petrol man,
they'd be too ashamed to show their face.
Plastic Fantastic?
PLASTIC FANTASTIC?
AYE RIGHT!!!

Graffiti Poem

Beyond watching eyes
With sweet and tender kisses
Our souls reached out to each other
In breathless wonder

And when I awoke
From a vast and smiling peace
I found you bathed in morning light
Quietly studying
All the messages on my
       phone

Do Not Say

Do not tell that I was here
passing through the woods;
do not say I stood and looked
upon a far-flung sea;
do not mention that you saw
me holding shadows in my hand
or slipping past black rivers
and talking with sharp crows.
Do not show that you know
that love is a rugged moon
or a yellow mist on marshland
or footprints in wet sand.

Do not say...
they will not understand.

IX

AFTER _____ that night a _____ endless drill of police and photo _____ _____ sby's from _____ a police-ma _____ kept out _____ urious _____ little boys _____ covered that _____ enter through my yard _____ Always a few _____ open-mouthed _____ e pool. Some-one with _____ positive _____ tive, used the expression _____ he bent over _____ s body that after-noon, and the adventitious _____ nity of his voice set the key for the newspaper rep _____ morning.

Most of those reports _____ nightmare – grotesque, circum-stantial, eager, and _____ en Michaelis's testimony at the inquest brought to lig _____ son's suspicions of his wife I thought the whole tal _____ shortly be served up in racy pasquinade – but Cath _____ ho might have said anything, didn't say a word. Sh _____ a surprising amount of char-acter about it too – l _____ e corner with determined eyes under that corrected _____ and swore that her sister had never seen Gatsby, _____ was completely happy with her husband that _____ een into no mischief what-ever. She convinced herself of it, _____ d cried into her handker-chief, as if the ve _____ re than she could endure. So Wilson was _____ nged by grief' in order that the case _____ remain _____ t form. And it rested there.

But all _____ ssential. I found

Homelessness

Walking these cold, lonely, London streets at night...
Not a soul in sight.
You feel so alone, on your own
No one to hold - cuddle up to at night.
Homeless, hungry, belly rumbling
Walk in the chicken shop
'Yo boss can you hook me up please? Man's homeless,
    hungry.'
'Come back at 2 o'clock.'
'OK! Sweet,' I'll keep walking
These lonely, London streets
Until my feet begin to bleed with blisters.
Keep 1 eye over my shoulder
For it's dangerous on these streets of London
AKA The Dungeon
Bossman hooked me up with
10 chicken drumsticks
Blessed
Just not feeling it
Homelessness ain't no joke
I seen some bloke
With his head in the bin
Looking for food
So I gave him mine
And went hungry for another night
I don't mind
It's the kinda guy I am
See next man happy
Makes me happy.
I'm a happy chappy kind of guy
Even though deep down I wanna cry
Mom and Dad's back in Guernsey

I'm all alone nowhere to go...
So I keep strolling these London streets.
Bumped into a yardie 3 for 2, that'll do.
Keep me going for the night
2 crack pipes
My eyes begin to rise
Fix up, look sharp
3 a.m.
Pitch black dark
Don't walk through Normandy Park
You get fucked for what you got
And what I got is my word and bond
I'll keep going on
Homelessness ain't no joke!

Panther 'X'

It was dark, everyone had gone. Panther pressed the
lock and the door swung open and the lights of the
town were like opium to him as he padded down the
road.

But he knew the danger was from the white man, so
he rested on the grass for a while. But he knew the
danger was from the white man. So he headed for the
mountains.

Panther was free;
Panther is free. And Panther will be free forever.

Bloom

Kindness is a virtue.

Words may be short, a couple vowels and a
few consonants but those words speak
infinities.

Kindness has so much power and it can
change the world.

The heart has vessels and those kind words
fill those vessels with daisies and
sunflowers.

Blooming at each beat.

And when nasty words are spoken, these
flowers wilt and turn dry, the petals
crumbling off into the bloodstream.

So water those vessels, keep the flowers
blooming.

Chain Poem

Countries all round the world in conflict and war
War that separates and causes hate
Hate that manifests itself in bullets, bombs and murder
Murder of the innocent and the guilty
Guilty as we turn over the news

Bookend II

The Old Worn Book

Sometimes I feel like an old worn book
With torn and tattered covers
Someone will take me down to read
But just pass me to another
My pages they will never turn
So how will they ever see?
All the chapters in my life
That's buried deep in me
If they don't read my story
How will they understand?
All the twists and turns in life
That's made me what I am
Next time you take me out to read
Don't pass me to another
Take time to look inside
And don't judge me by my cover

Koestler Arts

Koestler Arts (charity no.1105759) is the UK's best-known prison arts charity. Since 1962 the charity has inspired people in custody, on community sentences and on probation to transform their lives through the arts. The annual Koestler Awards generate over 7,000 entries across fifty-two categories including sculpture, film, music, painting, craft and poetry. Professionals in each field volunteer to judge the awards. Judges from 2022 and 2023 include Katie Piper, Rich Miller, and Bluebag Life, as well as former Koestler Awards entrants continuing their arts practice in the community. Entrants gain certificates and handwritten feedback, and can win cash awards, apply for mentoring or feature in exhibitions, events and publications.

Recent exhibitions include: *The Future Is Never Too Big*, a display of work by under 18s at the Supreme Court, London; *Our World*, co-curated by a group of Fife College learners from HM Prison Shotts, at Tramway, Glasgow; *On My Plate* in partnership with the *Doing Porridge* project at University of Surrey, at South Hill Park Arts Centre, Bracknell; and our sixtieth anniversary exhibition *Freedom*, curated by Ai Weiwei, at the Southbank Centre, London.

Each year the Koestler Awards inspire over 1,000 poems – making poetry one of the most popular categories. *Koestler Voices* is published biennially to provide a sample of this engaging and unique writing. Koestler Arts is grateful to the selected poets, all those who took part in the 2022 and 2023 Koestler Awards, and the people who supported and encouraged them to do so.

Supporters & Acknowledgements

Koestler Voices Vol. 4 would not have been possible without the support of everyone who joined our crowdfunding campaign. Thank you to each person who has helped further amplify the voices of writers in secure settings this year:

Jonathan A., Jonathan Aitken, Helen Aydon, Ariane Bankes, Rachel Barnes, Margaret Bechka, Annabel & Luke Blighfield, Jasmin Booth, Vicky Bowman CMG, Emma Buckmaster, Tom Campbell, Frances Carey, Dinah Casson, Alison & Simon Clements, Claudia Cotton, Nick Dent, Victoria Dickie, Wendy Dishman, Stephanie Donaldson, Anna Dowson, Andrea Edeleanu, Jill Edge, Heide Eyles, Cara Garven, Matthew Greenburgh, Henry Grunwald OBE KC, John Hewitt, Matthew Hobbs, Ian, Richard W. Ireland, Amber Jackson, Mel James, Daniel Jeffcote, Nikki Jeffcote, Peter Jeffcote, Kathryn, Michael & family, Peter J. King, Basia Korzeniowska, Fiona Larkin, Htein Lin, Margaret Lipsey, Thanh Ma, Margaret, Sarah Matheve, Alice May, Clare McGowan, Brendan McLoughlin, Elizabeth McVean, Rosy Meehan, Melanie, Caro Millington, Mary Angela Murphy, Shirley Nicholson, Ann Nunn, Jenny Oklikah, Olivia, Paul Pasquill, Theo Pigott, John Reiss & Freda Matassa, Caz Royds, Adrian Scrope, Peter Selby, Myra Silverstone, Eleanor Smith Communications, Philip Spencer, Richard Spencer, Sally Taylor, Sue Taylor, The Arts Society Hull & East Riding, Caroline Walker, Adam Walsh, Simon Wethered, Sue Whitley, Rob Williams, Christine Wong JP, Thomas Wynn, Sally Zimmermann, and all our supporters who have chosen to remain anonymous.

We would also like to say a huge thank you to our writing judges and feedback volunteers for sharing their time and expertise.